DAYS

DAYS

SIMONE KEARNEY

Belladonna* : 2021

DAYS © Simone Kearney

All rights reserved. First edition, 2021. Printed in Canada.
ISBN: 978-0-9988439-5-7
Book design by HR Hegnauer, typeset in Cardo and Century Gothic
Cover art by Simone Kearney

Belladonna* is a reading and publication series that promotes the work of feminist writers who are adventurous, experimental, politically involved, multiform, multicultural, multi-gendered, impossible to define, delicious to talk about, unpredictable, & dangerous with language.

This publication is supported by the New York State Council on the Arts, the Leslie Scalapino - O Books Fund, the National Endowment for the Arts, and donations from individuals. Belladonna* is a proud member of CLMP.

Cataloging-in-publication data is available from the Library of Congress

Distributed to the trade by
Small Press Distribution
1341 Seventh Street
Berkeley, CA 94710
www.SPDBooks.org

Also available directly through
BELLADONNA*
925 Bergen Street, Suite 405
Brooklyn, NY 11238
www.belladonnaseries.org

For every body crafts a recognition of its present or else disappears. LISA ROBERTSON

So writing is the method of using the word as bait: the word fishing for whatever is not word. When this non-word—between the lines—takes the bait, something has been written. Once whatever is between the lines is caught, the word can be tossed away in relief. But that's where the analogy ends: the non-word, taking the bait, incorporates it. So what saves you is writing absentmindedly. CLARICE LISPECTOR

oval in evening, body's little bad translator, like myself, about to begin, there, how this artichoke unfolds, clinging like a feeling at the end of sleep, scooped out of what grips, moving backward, forward, backward, forward, to get to the heart of the matter, heart of thing, leaf, oil, spring, light above my head crackles then swells, it is burning up, big as a balloon, block of morning in June, memory snags no connection, entering the world that hangs porously on morning, thread of life passes through me vertically and I feel it in me, pulling in opposite directions, growing repeatedly, elongating pause of missed corn or agapanthus, plastic, crop, rubber button, what I am doing, I only know how to construct small images I climb out of, it could almost be string, it is almost night, there is no man in it or woman, then in the dream there are rows of ancestors and friends, lovers, roots, rose, breath, faces moving up and down, wine-colored buffalo wings, windowless bibs of silence, a single dream can trace a contradiction, an internal one, like two arrows pointing at each other, unless contradiction isn't conflict, there, there, snouts stuck in cream, vying hole, what's on the radio, dig out pigments from ashtray, mouth is somewhere else, ant farm, bee nest, little eloping hairs, windows are forms of escape, off you go like a horse with your eyes swelling to pinpricks, horns that pierce the fine tunic of road air, I keep getting moved around by strangers' eyes, or they keep getting moved around by mine, they have no satisfying angles, no pure margin, I hear their humid speech, their chameleon words, borrowed, and there are fingers in them, similarly, gaps in place of the crotch, fog powder, where differences are hard to touch, unlatch, what is withdrawing, watershed, something pushing like a sun, up, since morning, venturing close to artificial shadows, watered down, me fizzing like a fig on a dashboard, sped up as a gun, I am getting shoved into all the weight of emotion, porphyry, knots tightly knotted, hills cut in half, I'm bored already, pretend to think about something else, pretend there is room for surprise, I start to remember your everything, wanting to explain the preliminary, dainty, reversible logic of a person, fences, hardly beginning, see yourself mounting stairs, color of sink, silences you lie in, what to do with words that stall, yielding to minor chunky unstitched landscapes, easily replaced, what does it mean to finish, trying to make sense of things, synonyms for rummaging through the length of a small, dried dot, as if wounds had etymologies, this is where you must live, hard to complete, derailed voice as clumsy athlete, polliwog under faucet, winter getting warm, it's easy to inherit a limp, e.g. Oedipus, deep absorbent open areas I walk over like puddles and I never have time, I'm always mopping up, I can't see what's moving, all this must appear as fireworks dissolving into façades, sandpipers in dunes, not knowing how to finish, particular word is a wasp, suppressed in cubicles, hours ago, breezes are everywhere, winter is a bundle of necks, I said to you, "sew me an ear's white drum," you plow words like water and arrive at the noiseless island of your throat, detached neighborhoods, I want to be free to ruin circles, this history of fluid doorways in night open like clay, it's boiling out, whatever is hidden is in those miniature bones of the neck, it is today, I thought it was a mauve vest, trees against trees, productions of surfaces that pour out of streets, when one's body doesn't fit one's head, grease covers my entire expression, many themes can be found in this face, and what words are folded inside your facial gestures, the face makes a sound of shrinking, there's a whittled beach, because it is blue skies again, blue scraped off the wheel, blue is scraped, everything tastes like soup, mistakes are points of departure, mistakes are catalysts for shape, for variation, multiplicity, if you look in a mirror you can see a whole list of your "mistakes" and "successes," such formations of accident are never neutral, though they exist alongside aggressive piles of adjectives and nouns they appear to never touch, absence of weight is a weight in and of itself, there is so much tingling going on, all around, it is damage, it is good damage, surface of this pink I see before me is damage, bits of living, what wrinkles out of rain, you wish you could be specific, like a policy of détente or a cracked jug, name is a vegetable slowly growing in my head, wasp gone, now words made of bees inside too much vegetable, it can be uncomfortable to hear for this reason, but one can't close one's ears, hands as useful as lids made of feathers in this regard, blowing, blowing, vegetable bee, all flapping, brain in thought can be old wallpaper peeling away to reveal even older layers, those layers can be folded into geometric shapes that have no value except to reveal depth, which even paper can betray, sky like contents that's been looked at too many times, sky has been passed through a machine, sky is the remainder after it has been used, is whitish after so much use, I will be aloof, shapeless, demanding, plateau of shrill feeling, this is how you do it, we are getting closer, at our usual places, the obvious analogy is with a person, who, washing the windows, vanishes in glass, relationships move like suspicious playthings, like a memory with its meaning diluted into language, like the limit of a digression, baggage we carry, perpetual history, and memory up on a wall, what we had hoped for, as if we could trap ourselves, definite as background music, I like materials that grip, the world is true and real, or is it real and true, the difference in the order of operations, your arms are strings of water, your arms are unequal shawls, stairs in water, door's milk, something is touched we don't know, everything is entire and slips, morning grit, cloud straying from some stopped sunned turf, that was before you washed and rose, felt objects vaguely coming into focus, objects you only know to place side by side, sun on knees, names came to me like a mirror facing the wrong way, names dangling out of themselves like the end of Wednesday, PowerPoint eyes, when considering relationships between two inanimate objects, the human element keeps bursting in on the scene, its intrusion of cake-orange, greenish tension between ropes that are almost flesh, how the skin of things keeps getting interrupted, meanings grow fuller and burst, grapes, sack of shared memory that, once touched, makes you the same as everybody else, then dissolves, free in the silence of its rearrangements, sometimes cages are comfortable, sometimes absence is a cage, sometimes an object beats like the size of a voice, sometimes there is the delayed reaction of a burn evening out a thinness of feeling, drops of feeling make their way to you slowly, like the light of old, rough stars, so that my feet are light and I race, glaze of things without closure, stars like boxes oozing, and I treat words like boxes too, ones with folding parts made of glass, too clear even when folded up, too clear, the way glass is blown, wobbles, falls down, arthritic light, opaque as sting ray, as air, like Ruth, who stood amid the alien corn, and now history is rearranging the garment of itself, the garment is no more, or rather is something else, how to read it, if I could wipe away my own hand, and everything is almost graspable, night, Dunkin', and in the window, nothing filters through, nothing appears other than the room, walls, wind getting up, wavering, as if it could attach itself to a voice, kale breath, so many promotions bloating the whole head of you, and night trying to gather a solid, aloof verb, almost complete, Twinkie shimmer, to form a phrase, cylindrical and scooped, you use your exquisitely controlled mouth, like a scar on fruit, Bonne Maman plum dropping dark red on toast, such discovery is perceptible, distance thrown on you like warm cloth, worrying about lockjaw, mosquito buzzing on a split fig but actually it's a Honda that splashed your slippers, not even shadows at angles with people itching in cul-de-sacs, this wall of language that blocks speech, in the shop, handing out, in silence, what's at my disposal, blank absorbent tissue, *flatus vocis*, and other realities, presses into you, fact remains, I'm thrown into spectacles of words, collaged, even in my foreign tongue, stone, egg, when day moves, raw as lard, cashew milk, the sound of portraits, noise before one can talk, sleep was lost in a room, little airplane spotted over Internet, making no progress, certain fingers in the margin, procedures, where you can't linger, oof or woof, only leaves, grounds, but not phones filled with transactions, approaching a reflection out of doors, I could sail to a life of imitations that never occurred, a kind of burbling, fuchsia, agate jelly, animal in the open, kind of calf, scrappy hairdo, funky houses bubbling up like mushrooms then torn down, vulnerable fungi gill, that window, and then you want to FaceTime, pour your life into one on screen, you are in a room too large to hide everyone's vocabulary sizzling away, something shredding when we talk, rounding, river, mull, kind of thing, standstills of mouths, another wrong impression, pushing, white bleeding squeezed into tusk-clean apertures, such compulsions as the need to violently fade, go poof, masquerade invisibly like space or power, where a mask of air punctures, as that gossamer would, but then there is also the need to puff, to spill out onto surfaces, smear volumetric spheres of one's body, ladle out onto lawns, over an armchair, onto the ottoman, over the TV, through the carpets, onto someone else's presence, onto the cup of their beautiful hand, their care, the little rivulet of their need, the dent they need filling, somewhere in the background of sentiment narrowed to irrelevance, she said, in other people's gardens, worn, sky, a tad overcast, cloud, glue, one to another, after is before, progeny of lisps, joint prosody to make rubber odes, something is being blown out, you're doing the trope thing again, you're following a line, red herring, tape, footsteps, something being diminished, traps you can hear, something thrust into its own stillness, something about remaining alert, something about not standing on the yellow line, something self-capitalizing, something residual on top, something sagging in waterholes, shuddering on a broken fluorescent corner, pillaging veins in an open field, dumb and leather, resurfacing, pouring a tunnel, but if flowering were there, what's clipped, nounless, coagulating light, stalking a series of unspecified dead ends, pressed into nubs of atmosphere, touch someone else's inhalation, I'm sitting on a feeling as if sitting on a chandelier, iffy, hunger is sticky, I touch you like

an object that disappears into the sound of tearing, I touch you like a hill in midnight
I'd escaped, hours packed round your hair, a hand, give it to night just once, tomorrow,
nettle path, thin stone, bees empty of time touching consonants, grooves that unfold,
syllable by syllable taken off into grass shadows, crystal on foghorn, the life I read,
make your place in the faces of others, cold but erotic, speaking into your hand that
is not a telescope, and we know where we're going, or where we should go and then
we are everywhere, blurs, permanent as matter, writing at the computer, to become

grammarians of sweet Amyctis' body, I am full, feeling full, features on sun, moon has more features actually, sneers, or as if about to sneeze or keen, salt and pepper, eyes without pupils, no eyeballs, just smudges like turf mounds seen in the distance like thongs, crying patches, all the ways in which nature is animal, nature is human, and then swallows the human, absorbs it like its own blood, poor or rich, all of us roaming in our clothes like divots, like bumps with mirrors coming out of them, and the moon is a trickle of light and there is no grief on it, that was just an image, flash in the pan, skinny, poking through a piece of cloud and the cloud smudges the light like a snail trail, in the morning, the snails got over everything, snails of light, light, light, I was too shy to speak in front of the crowd, my friend got bored with me, wouldn't speak to me, I am bullish change, she thinks to herself, triplets of weeds, she exfoliates, flip-flopping traffic of lips, this bruise on paper, brand new soap, I think it's vegetarian, made of pears, I circle around, or back, this flag that could smother you if you're not careful, dragonfly landing on your eyelashes, sun, sun, so much sun, then blue to dark again until the sun comes and then the grey comes, I am cool fissures, grass growing lushly, root that ran down to the pond, rain you almost detected, how detached rain is, falling from the source, how we, too, shed away, sort of mise-en-scène, synthetic unscripted moments, or if bodies are imprecise constructions, I'm okay with that, reviling the viscosity of being near you, desiring, browse your violet arrow, edible nasturtium, structure of me, you, putty, tough, become more, fix my face, laugh behind chin, *vous êtes un chien mordu*, we're almost shot through, proportionate to crumbling hair on a soaked My Little Pony, favorite doll, are ponies dolls, there is an art in being humanely dismantled you think as you write texts, it demands a sly action, like picking apart a bird lung or stem cell under scrutiny, magnified, words in a squint, which ones to dissolve into like landscapes of wet cement where a mold has prematurely been taken away, diameters in place of walls, someone's so-so cousin of a face, full of fresh ends in a canal, October no one remembers, also, suspension of early evening in the head, emotions water, cloud water, rabbit hole, pet vulva, faces soft as emulsified Béarnaise sauce, *et ton doigt sur la brute, Capitaine!*, terror in flesh, poke me, what parts stretched into cloud, naturally into the nascent smell of sap, obvious avenues, grass-stuffed, owl hole, calls, eroded whenever you said my name, whatever you said absorbed there slowly, slowly she moved towards him, and, with head bowed, watched the huge doll of his body, and your name draws me like fire, and what, on the other side, is not, in this moment, finished, "I will not eat," and go on humming quietly and halfway back, necks pulled in, utterly mismanaged, swoosh, so what, go on, go on, gate building music, mobility is in a sense forced on us, plying our horizons, Girl Scout handbooks, in any case it was no longer my house, that too was a melancholy matter, such as night and day, syrup on bread, "it's a word, it doesn't look like one, but it is," I was coming back from the day, sprawled as a hide, I was finishing it, squeezing handkerchiefs, the outer part of your eye conceals the inner part, and every orifice crumples, what your face says is aggressive, and then it ebbs into stillness, stillness of arranged furniture, showy, or then again, snap, everything offered up, where, floating reflection flashes on and off like an expression of promise that gets obscured behind a sneeze and with that everything collapses and then gets rearranged, the face I mean, hard to translate, what animal is this, to diagram, shapes ferment into foam, contracts like traffic, it is soon dry, it does not blink with sense, because I am around my mouth, tiptoe of water and I lie, lie in water, and beside me, I put my clothes, where's the start, ribbon of finishing, polish, congestion, stop then start, memory taped to back of sky, dream-sized voice on skyscrapers and bungalows, aloud, views of my walls, lobby fogs up, baby volcanoes, when you look, earth's orifice, my mouth, there, in the hotel, windpipe blowing like herbs, we must use the body in the proper way, air curls into folds, I keep falling in this way, salt water ebbs, "her silence is her power," says Ariana, it's me talking now, it's February, inert violent soft clue, scratching, horny, dripping, subdued, smoking, waiting for something to happen, neckline of woman, sleep's first hugeness of tint, just inches above sea level, cloud keeps layering, first a steamy dirty kind, then a soggy trim kind, windows are like televisions, plumb spang in the cow-creamer, writing has been a little cage too, natural paper eyes, bleach the places in which one used to see words, or fill it with earth, water, echo, those marble statues firm and polished, put a rainbow on it, distant from my mother tongue, I mangle what I'm left with, not settling for life, the quality of a feather's shortness, describable as nails, grains, resolution inside volume, I know love, trying to see others' eyes, what can sustain itself, not wanting, evolving heart in diagrams, picturing my semilunar valves, gestures that flake off me like a discrete tumescence, produces a single repeatable action, what will you do, the precision of passivity, how it congeals into form, hard anonymous void an eye fills when open, puffy, still clouded by the inside parts of darkness, total body of vision tending towards peripheries of feeling, something waiting to be formulated where light piles, interior snow floors, no one's face is here yet on seams of speech, vision is a bandage, prattle is a drape, islands of blank arguments, I see big corners, postures seeping, clarity, hooded, residues, blot, blob, wet, pane, commas, like hats on the sea, tucking in the ooze of world like a belt, and I unbelt the word, no, put the belt on, comma is shell, word is shell, as in egg, as in torn-open sea, I know what you mean says the man holding my hair momentarily, I know exactly what you mean, to look outside and touch another finger, not a cold one but a hot one in the dunes, these things don't come together, a bitter shot goes limp in the waist, this is what it means to be animal and wrist, chartreuse, nest in trees, place for walking, this is what you could do, or how it begins, slow water, recollection, day, this part on display, burst of quietness fitting into hours, irregular opal miming a second language, on the side of roads, lines wandering somewhere else, and all these fences blotted out, but reappearing, and again, since she is also a moral space like everybody else, yes, she thinks, one can always show oneself off, potato spice, beyond the pale, mistaken notion that the palate encloses noises of other apartments, instead, this is a site of suffering that has the silhouette of twig, like the fact of skin, place each one side by side, little sexless accidents of history, compact as accent, as short-rib, blurt, silence, corners of a mouth that move from pale magenta to aquamarine are slopes of hill until she swallows, other sound floats forward noiselessly, seamlessly, or hops like a three-legged dog in the ear, elsewhere the chatter of men in the other room became hoards of undiluted smoke or hair, whose, in the room in which she sits and thinks, makes an image of, inside, and the mouths on screen, herself fogging up, squashed into a mirror, close, particular, and concrete, a promise, properly speaking, of a face, she is her own wee helper, "her protrusions her gifts," she a kind of nude without need for organs, she like a painting she would have read about, neither inside nor outside, nostalgia for grass, trait of Bacon, greasy though cerebral, analogical enough to be language, injected with mutilated fact, sensation is broken like a rhythm, amplified mother-of-pearl doused in flesh and nerve until it bounces back with a spasmodic appearance and falls again, as if a body with no outsides could surface, angular convulsion in large armchair, or hysterical contour in washbasin, this is the threshold, this is the domain, the tenor of its muscle, of its organic form, limpid friction against steam, chiaroscuro breaking off from itself, like a bird alighting on a field, space without form, vast intellectual straining, going in opposite directions, gel-like apparition, it is, hair laid out like a displaced taste, partition is dots, image gone loose, drink, body, if only I were a red sun, lifted up as pieces of furniture, *pièce détachée*, it is the story you told about, extreme point in a face lingers in air like an ant on a beer's rim, luminous on the eye, seeing, knowing, feeling, the operation through which something contracts like a parachute, dying to escape, crouched mouth, creasing its secret, garland in trough, manual space, I'm cushioned by what I see, perception's a horn, friction against steam, motionless foreground, all these aspects, of course, coexist in reality, I no longer think in any other way, specifically optical, self is fork through mousse, coagulated porch, about to flare, inedible, cognition parts like tributaries of fat, no longer ascending like a life, I could go on and on in a rut, night's chair, or covert, stumped, and risen again, it is normal, then, all this doing only to undo, or undoing to do, foul, human, or useless stone, subject in mangled sentence like a ditch with no sides, arouse sound in what you feel like saying, now what you said has a dumpling shape, overcast, mishmash of meaning that could have been a figure split by this subway glint, or, I was there, I wanted to answer, and did, taut and clammy on the platform, everyone stood like a tree, your head can be a funnel, exchanged for strange nubile water, water of a life, give your head smelling of cheesecloth to another, strained thoughts, don't let them touch you on your way out, eye is a hot ditch, fondue of seeing where matter starts to melt, to become delectable, as for other signs, all the ideas shrivel like violets in a hospital, mood slender as background or curled-up shrimp, almost a text, a little more than one, an exegesis of glass, his face was a pumice stone, shadows nested inside each pore, little warm wells, but then got released again and tumbled out, hump full of space like water sloshing around, and you love as you would bunched psychological space that nevertheless has the aura of physical scent, what fits into the angle of each feature, full of cause and effect, leaves behind a feeling of having felt, that's her left hand, it simplifies in the light of day disrupted as collage, reattaching like a doodad to the body, social body, immune, still, writing is a method, good or bad, towel of selves mopping up all the skin of life, skin of others, skin of voices, skin of heartbeats, sweat, cum, come, skin of all the music, all the music, toweling itself, what shows us otherwise, spheres of voices, all the spheres of beings, fragile, agile, opaque, so full, come near, come with me, here, here you are, there, here is all this rich dirt in which things grow, all the moisture of flowers, all the flowers flooding the atmosphere with red, blue, and yellow, oily in air, yes, she dreams of entering germs like history and making agriculture out of it, no logical position can account for the semantics of a body, its bones are tiny prisms, chunky light, imitations of knots that keep undoing, they contain too much of what is more than their size, sudden understanding of words turned inside out, badly done where flesh is indicated as question, strictly speaking, why can't you move more fluidly, why can't you be moved fluidly, my poor vehicle, sponges up ideas of herself, one by one, isolated as the wing of a pigeon, fetishizing her own exclusion, when thinking starts to float up like parts of a face into other people she wishes she were, forefinger and thumb, they are nubs of animal fat melting into thumbprints, they could have been bullets, this is identity, every person could be an instrument, sometimes eroding the idea of a vowel that keeps stretching outwards into a plank, but at its end is something more shallow, a straw, you imagine you are squeezed into the tiniest hole of who you think another person is, then the hole expands, here I am, you are seen by another as through the light of a porthole, voice, gesture, and scent balled together, voice-ball bounces, and this is how communication happens, this ball melts, over to the other side, person, place, or thing, say it, enigma of world like a heating pad you perch on, soft testimony gets softer, just to be around, enigma's pant, enigma of tongue, of hard body, or soft, balloon-skin, question of how to arrange anything after trauma, words always require that they be arranged like objects on a windowsill, otherwise meanings can't arise, tell your story, one, two, three, four, five, six, already damaged by time, time, just in an everyday sense, in a mundane way, you feel that if you uttered a word, it would slowly crumble inside you in turn, like the doppelgänger of the same word you uttered, it's falling to pieces there, a kind of decay of word inside you, lodged, broken apart like spumes wilt, everything that was both simple and double at the same time, what you said, it is there in your memory like goo on the portion of an action you want to perform, finger your voice, Anna said she would explain something to me, she's gone to get milk, vernacular scars, exit, abstract spittle, gauze of speech covers you as warming milk forms a skin, how abjection works, you read about, voice a thing in your mouth, not knowing where to attach, who to attach to, that voice smells of rejection, you want to touch it as if it were a parent, paddling you towards a destination that's not a destination meant for you, you were supposed to go the other way, but you are abominably passive, I found this in an email Charlie had written years ago, an idea can have no corners, it can resemble a propeller in a meadow, no one knows how it got there, but you are sitting in your chair, only imagining things, an image erupts to compensate, and with talking, despite it all, the apparatus of them, what you can't understand or write down is lump in blankets, this is too dramatic, to dramatize incommunicability, how then could anyone communicate anything, and yet they do, look at this report, where would we be without it, at least it's a stab at justice, fails often but other times it's real vindication that can alter the visible, so structures start to wobble and sometimes reshape, undone completely, built up again in a different direction, ghost-blobs, pass the meringue, this can be the beginning of something, rupturing, gloss over books in the therapist's room, I count them one by one to avoid my fate, or my lack of fate, either option is to be avoided, Rona looks far away, as if in rain, she's amazing, you look at her as through corrugated glass, see yourself through that textured glass of her eyes as if your own voice or desire or rage were some large, opaque blip, undone completely, sometimes, suddenly it's not her and her coarse transparency, or yes, she's glassy, but more opaque than you think, or in fact she's not like glass at all, she's mirroring your words back to you, turning them into glass for you, the process is uncomfortable, focus as purchased, greedy, sponging up the gaze, you both watch, that's a rosy rhombus of enormous rosy glass exiting my mouth, . . . , not unlike wool prisms, facets too dense or thin to scatter, each facet winds around your tongue like a spool, you feel rich, you feel rich, spin a yarn, go for it, story of your life, plumb line, words drop from your tongue like exquisite eggs, you, you are the hen, my love, you are the hen, lay, lay your words down, friends, and my love, what moves across, space you reside in, as single dew, thinking to yourself, what pressure of filament that moves across your face to mine, all the books of us, all the labor and density, the trespassing, the receding, the denial, the giving, the telling, the sharing, like this root of feather, not being able to tell the difference between the true and the false, where the body is, for the feather to come from, for words to come from, from where, and how, to be shared or known, stones, pseudonyms, at the stand, eating ice-cream, it's vegan, you wouldn't know it, you brought me there, we winced, it rains, what is this tendency, putrefaction of the mind, tits perky in t-shirts, others soft smoke, you would love a red coat, blue jeans, I am trying to fit into your face, gutters of water, pump, seahorse, steam stiffened into stalactite like diphthongs rolling down amygdalas, closed, open, I am a book, something sounds like something else, giggle in the hedge instead, trail of weather pops out, I'm on the inside of a bird jacket, embedded bird, a symbol for potential, duck, I am dreaming of subjects that have lost their magnetism, two days and a half ago I left, bumping up against what's visual is numb, Lycra jumpsuit, dwell in your bed and wait for your birth, I pierce it, pictures burst, then more pictures, holes, holes of mementos, souvenirs, with a wiggly mustache above the hole, almost on fire, slick as otters' tails, pushed into the backs of sentences, banshee, imported tail, she placed her tongue where no center occurs, she liked them because they were beautiful, they were, who she could call beautiful in a deep sense, and their voices were beautiful, and their hands held her like she was a living cylinder, and their voices met like brief retina catching light in nets, an exchange of information, thigh gap size, all the ocean of meeting, a corner entry, porridge of silence, splotches of gorged mauve, she told one of the strangers who was not looking at her, consciousness is disheveled verb, or residue, badly slurped oyster, mine and yours, out the window, on the train, in the street, in the gutter, in the trash can, in the house, in the cranny, under the bridge, sprawled like a fume on a finish line, or woven into one endlessly dense reel, blankets of appearance, secrets on arms, playground with dirt, plastic grass was "planted" around it, now it's out the window, something sludgy, repaved into the form of healed scars, a kind of half-way house of recognition, or I jump over that train of thought and see a container with a tissue covering it, when I remove the tissue, I look into the container, there's a feeding tube which is attached to a nonvascular flat scale-like cell, like single-crystal silicon, but made of something more like spirit, clearly a significant base material, from which other discrete components emerge, how they are free of boundaries, meant to disperse thought like conductors, lapel of atmosphere, squeeze, controlled like a serum as if coming through a syringe, and what is this hand again but shape in curd, cognition parts like tributaries of fat, no longer ascending, thinking is enough, you are monocle, your seeing moves ahead, but where is the bottom of sensation, of origin, could you hold it like a tool, garden hose, Lisa in the garden with leaves, stalk's allure, doing sweet things to the whole, face an incipient bud of someone else's history or idea as much as your own, or lie down, take it, what you write, how the gesture of writing is the motion of brooms sweeping towards or away from an incubator, mounds of images, cooped up, un-hatched, write in your long inky handwriting with flourishes around the "y" so that the tail of the "y" curls back on itself and pierces the "o" like a thing in an arena, skewered-like-a-heart-bleeding-all-over-the-place-of-an-"o," writing "I" is sometimes like touching your own genitals in public, you write, writing "I" is like being stuck inside a life-sized cream cheese sandwich, plops down on couch, intelligence unzips like a onesie, what's left, weather on piles of glens, for instance, Bobby yelled at you, you yelled back, you hugged, here was, this is another word for sexuality, I put the sexuality in a casing, closed object that is nevertheless geometrically proportionate to openness, unique as a comb, or then on it, as in, in, its surface, sort of, "you" is there, smiling, yes, but for the rest, surfaces, plankton, or that which is not yet ostensible, that (which?) is always still conditional, away, take me home, all the lapping, everything starts to un-wedge, I have sensation, the day traverses me so that I am beside, personal surfaces I hide under to protect myself from the social order, bobbing in depth, did you see the way the waves are grasses, Misty and Jay show me the way pea pods climb walls, well in the background and a goat, but the ego is compressed so that imagination is on either side of it, yanking something out with forceps, I wonder what has been written inside the space like a cloud, could be cloud of something that replaces legibility, cloud that denies access, if you removed the cloud, maybe you too would be removed, keep looking for erect language, in order to use grammar effectively, put the "t" before the "u" etc., hard to remember, *Les Règles Du Jeu, jeux*, no, without the "x," all the musk of writing, the tips of my fingers are oversensitive, no image at all, let's face it, never seen as it actually is, ideas are objects, dress them up, or dress in them, layer, watery, osmosis of assignations, word is clothing too, artifice, mask, fabric, surface, as in this sea, hem supplants the face, I feel all hem today or yesterday, first it should be known that the shirt is dense with seams, but may be cleansed, I've always found hygiene suspect, language can be a cleaning utensil, a surgical one, scalpel of language is sometimes useful in times of oscillation, clean cut of description, remove the fray from fact, go, rhymes with, then it's mess, say something clearly, cleanly, some light has been shed on my emaciation, for instance, I now understand that the blockage of my ability to be is an inability to take in, intake, imbibe, absorb, I push out with my weak eyes, nothing but air pushes into me, I'm externalizing myself, handing myself out like a canteen given to no one but to promote instead the opposite of intact borders, you must have a contour to function, why fucking could be threatening, and risks abstracting you, why it is also alluring, to vegetate ecstatically almost outside of yourself, the effect of heat is the same, how it erases borders, cold does the opposite, compresses you inward, in the heat though you expand all your horizons into more horizons and suddenly you are the edge of a chair, or a piece of food on that counter, but on the other hand, cold numbs you until you are neither outside nor inside too, or a release from the things of yourself, here, in front of the sea, let your ear be pudgy of sea, with, out, as in exhale, where are you, slowly, and what, on the other side, is not, in any case it was no longer, my house, peanuts on cream, air curls into a tiny fold, it's me talking now, cloud, smearing windows, unpruned, pruning, still clouded by other inside parts, total body of vision tending towards peripheries, I know what you mean says the man holding my hair momentarily, I know exactly what you mean, to look outside and touch another finger, this is what it means to be, and to continue to operate, as though in a sequence or continuous trajectory, astonished for a little while with elasticity, imagine, silhouette of your head trailing off after lunch, unto whom alle wille spekith, and unto whom no privé thing is hid, expand your horizons into more horizons and suddenly you are the edge of a balcony, shavings, plugging up holes, something grows over something else, desire to fall headlong, threshold of swoon, wish to organize it in a certain way, bleary sorts of rectangles, triangles will also do, I have a threesome, take everything literally, sandpaper everything, remain stable, quit, annoy people, treat others obliquely, tend towards isolation, or I'm incredibly social, put on my clothes, sit down, the sound of my thought is the sound of a snail sliding up the smoothest eerie stone, "Get up," where's the start, random time constraint, sudden gurgle in the tummy made one stop in one's tracks, gaps curdling, grey radio, still blurred by other insides, the under blurs, realize that out of redness a mealy blue trickles in (or fails to), ears, padlocks, language is at the bottom of punishment, years spread out on your face, cooked turnip sky, to find something has shifted, slightly, heads wafting in and out of rooms, Lucy, June, everything submitting to matter, to escape, thought is creepy, think instead of stringy landscapes, recognizing there the face, features start to drift away, this survival of images, impregnated with memory-images, frustration of trying to find a thing with no middle, adjusts, what/who sponsors, when two things are precisely alike, and, simultaneously, point to one another, there is sometimes a breaking point and they become unrecognizable one from the other, as though mutilated by nearness, offices of bearded pasty attires, even as they are intact, lose their identity, stripe of oatmeal white against a flap of cartilage-white against gooseberry-white, background blowing at our heads, *an bocht 's an nocht go docht 'san mheala*, where there is no water there is also drifting, history becomes a chafe from the braille under your senses, inside words, or outside, *degens*, like your pants are too tight and short, exit the Gap, mind sharpens on the borders of each object it rubs up against, dreaming of Laura Ashley, a kind of nightmare, fatty with place inside the shape that I am if you look at me close up, who decides, *Yoga Magazine*, and who is you, is it you or is it me, but do I really love you, do I love Mel, do I love Trish, do I love Frankie, do I love Paul, I'm not sure, it could go either way, he sometimes says he loves me, but then he starts to whimper or laugh, and I can't tell what that means, is this a joke, I held her hand in the rowboat, tossed our heads back so the sky looked underwater, more savory than honey, like a steam room at the Y, steam rising and rising like a sun, we couldn't tell the difference between need and love, need became love and then love became need, we're hoping to cultivate a good type of affection, now I'm back in the apartment, I'm walking on the Thames, she also met her husband on the Thames, Wittgenstein knew that the "same" in "same river" is not quite the same as the "same" of "I have the same pain you have," for how can I judge the intensity of your pain, I read about this, continue reading others, about the nonreferentiality of the hurt body, and all the waves, the sea, the sea, where is your head with little choices, granola, here is pomade of uncertainty, stung as, chomp, as I go there I realize that day only wants things done to it, it doesn't want to do anything to anything else, it doesn't want to move a thing, it doesn't want to push an object out of place to give it a new place, it just wants the world to shape it because it can't shape itself, it doesn't want to be responsible for shaping other things, it wants to be made of, it wants world to make off with it, clearly this is projection as I sit on a couch and refuse, fusion, if only, verbiage cruddy on sleep, I wipe away my cognizance of this heartbeat in my body like a correspondence I erased, I pull violets, bee dust, bee stem, woozy, all over the rotation of each limb, so that there are no more letters, in Paris I was incredibly neurotic, alone, other days I stared at fireplaces, drank rum and read Homer, retention of mentality, its dual status growing on the hinge of a collective voice constituting a border that wants to be a property, "whose?", we, were/we're, our hour has come, this is as clear as it gets sometimes, but still, what is it to emerge, can you see that I'm emerging, like a root, she pricks the earth, I read about emergence, or what has only partially emerged, emerged from where, on my way to work, if the whole of language were present to me when I spoke, then I would not be able to articulate anything at all, trundling forward, being trundled, landscape of signs, Peter Pan, Port Authority, Regular Credit, Regular Cash, Retail Opportunity, Club Feather, Total Wine & More, J & Co Hair, NetCost Market, Mantra, Bahama Breeze, Blick's Art Materials, Red Lobster, Smashburger, Perfect Pawn, Metropolitan Plant And Flower Exchange, you're it, swing sets, light, waves, lighting, Once Upon A Child, Peter Crotty, FedEx Office,

Pearl Art Tiger, Suburban Golf, Galaxy, Spirit, concept, emergency exit, push window, Tea Neck, Hertz, Shoes Capital, Globe, Nord, Papa Razzi, Parking, No Stopping Or Standing, F79CWD, M57ARU, Do Not Enter Racetrack, everybody's talking 'bout the stormy weather, East, Coach, USA, Tiger Mart, Dermatology Next Right, Shop Dollar, Ikea, Open, Wells Fargo, Kmart, The Goods, EMS, Barnes and Noble, The Goodwill Store, Popeyes, Booksellers, Equinox, Guitar Center, E-topia, saddle, river, no turning, Signature Leather Furniture, Sale, Whole Foods, Key Food, Regal Foods, Breakfast,

Pizza, Expert Infertility Care, We Buy Ugly Houses, 212-744-44-11, RX, Community Jackpots, Dentist, Natuzzi, West, Fairway, GNC Live Well, Lighting Superstore, Patio.com, All American Collision Center, Citibank, Toys "R" Us, JoS. A. Bank Clothiers, T-Mobile, spirit desire, spirit, Benjamin Moore, Fitness Equipment, Airsoft Tactical Sports Authority, face me, Staples, Superstore, The Vitamin Shoppe, DXL, Verizon, Babies "R" Us, America, Proud To Be Among America's Best, Crate And Barrel, Aladdin Smoke Shop, Cartridge World, desire, miss me, Petco, Sleepy's, Marburn Curtains,

Value, we will fall, Beal, AT&T, LensCrafters, Super Center, Dollar Tree, BJ's, DJ's Express Entertainment, Auto Body, Lukoil, Tiger Mart, Tile Shop, S.E.A., Fitness and Wellness, Home Depot, Exxon, Satin Dolls, Crystal Clear, Stop and Shop, Carvel, Chit Chat Diner, Friendly's, spirit desire, spirit desire, we will fall, Fribble, Guaranteed Credit Approval!, Hilton, BP, Bazaar, America's Finest Self Storage, Fabric Outlet, Horizon, Porcelanosa, Olive Garden, Hardwood, Electric Car Wash, Extreme Care, The Bottle King, Hertz, Chili's, Chipotle, Visions Federal Credit Union, The Container Store, Wawa,

Plumbing and Heating, Wayne Tile, WURTH USA Inc., Double Tree, Cartridge World, Comfort Suites, Grand Buffet, DICK'S Sporting Goods, Trader Joe's, Shake Shack, Best Buy, Party City, The Fireplace, spirit desire, we will, Equinox, McDonald's, Starbucks, Ski Barn, Shell, BellAqua Inc., QuickChek, Extended Stay America, Uncle Giuseppe's Marketplace, State Line Diner, Mason Jar, that was my commute, what about progress, I had no clue, what of desire, it, steamroll, fall, feel euphoric, walk around a museum, stare at the white space, that gap grows into a lump, later in the day, to conceal one act with another act, and all the dust will drift away, murk, this, then this, wheat from chaff kind of thing, but what about the Statutes of Kilkenny, one example, no foible, peel the skin off the apple, slow, its difference, not bare, sweet angular taste, to press nouns into shapes watered down, pull them out like webs, to multiply the person that is a remnant of a person, it is constrictive, it is beautiful, sat down on the only chair in the room, postponed packing his box for the time being, since the whole night still lay before him in which to do it, but why do you stay here if they treat you like that, my words, glycerin spread on windows so I couldn't see out, in terms of intervals, they can be seen as rivers with logs drifting on them, what happens when enough of them float by, there it goes, or put another way, every time a person bumped into me I felt either the equality or inequality of diameters, pocket of distance, deep fleecy Uniqlo, relationship of distance to complicity, incipient flower, immoral, the nucleus, like Wittgenstein talks about, the difference, or rather, the interval, measure each other's intervals, this wad of interval, made dense as an organ, aura of density, like a lung filling with water, interval in the shape of a clock that got demolished, but the pieces of it float all over the place, pause between your nose and mine, like a rod in a marathon, hand me a rod, a cod, I mean cone, everything implanted to an outside, you can't go in, *nacio*, mark my words, sagging underbody of words, words we cling to like a wall, *Transactions of the Royal Historical Society*, way of life and speech, do you see this same mind start to occupy air that isn't tight enough, puckers, wicker, kite, beet, smoothest hands, coating, lines the sides of everything it's near, that coat, I went home, I don't know, what undoes the form, that's me crouching in a field, or a diagram of need, mental impotence, forms a glob in the mirror, embodying itself fluidly, submitting to itself like to a pimp, brush teeth, wash face and brush hair, wear pants for work, now mouth opens and thinking floats up to the face, take this spoon, while you say something to Olaf who asks you to paint words made out of wood, you stoop over the word "What?" in your shorts, rainwater filling up a concave object until the object was so full it spilled out of itself, breaking the form, but I've said this before, can you hear yourself, longing for a burger, could stop at the bistro with the cute flashing sign, where to place my eyes except on the cucumber on the plate beside me, feeling of mayonnaise, I sense the woman's temple throbbing next to me from the corner of my eye, I feel the thinking spot near the ear, its silence, not to defeat, not to squander, I have no socks, I dangle meticulously my left toe until all the oxygen bathes it like a parent, no one sees this under the table, I'm wearing flip-flops, sitting in Aideen's bed watching *Blue* by Jarman, voice on a stream, to be rooted is perhaps the most important and least recognized need, as if we understood matter, dermal, ground,

vascular, aerial or aerating, non-leaf, non-nodes, infilled voids, casts, sadness become
thinginess, dull name where loss of memory is, nose dives, forward into day, hour, what
about lines in Bertolucci's *Conformist*, when I see light coming through shutters, space
not neutral but skewered by idea, everything an idea of something, word for something,
if architecture, art, design, all forms, are ideological, everything birthing, birthed by idea,
dissecting the world, but the world never was, it is this, here, when, grey, actually grey,
matter, but not, or is it someone else's navel, or is it aloe vera that is simply in a jar,

jarring, unravel, what it is to circle, for all the cooling necessary of a mystical body, can't process, I wonder what this woman thinks of me, she thinks I'm an idiot, but I never tire of looking at you, often I don't know who you are, but I imagine you, you are somewhere inside the apartment of a person sometimes who says "I am much too much," "I am much too little," examining the curious shift of an assertion depending on the context in which it occurs, as in, on this landscape, dying leaves, wincing, puppies, parent's raw breath, I keep showering, or outside the car, a tree, a tree blowing, left, then right, holding a baby that looks like a fruit, you turn away, you have the head of a horse and the body of Cromwell in 1653, I want to tell this to you, I had been a shipbuilder building a boat on its way to a melting snowball at the port, I just woke, memory is that hill over there, sinking, your voice like graffiti on an icecap, icosahedron or truncated cube, in a room, this split hair lifting off the ground, "I really like you," like a bee stuffed with its stripe, bound into a ball, one can be stuffed with too much lightness until one's body becomes no longer body but thing, Dr. Pepper, in a diner in Wyoming, teenagers, I haven't washed my hair, and all the sea like expectations of beautiful longing, you slipping into pools, like some head rolling out a carpet onto a sheet, all red, flower-red, it's not enough to feel, there's too much sheets, rain drapes the outside and inside of the window because from here I can't tell the difference, we stay in a motel, the red dessert, I mean desert, is hidden in the darkness, we'll have to wait, words, "I agree," prodding, gel of ginger, shredded wheat, and is that your face, mounted onto thought like some oozy hill, there are flowers there, and grasses, what's the difference between a head and a face, all the subjective lengths of a length, *zut, je suis naz, je suit, je suis un* nōz, *un nez, por favor, itter bitter eine kleine Nachtmusik*, follows, and starts to press inwards, sometimes, a dog jumps up on your vanity, he doesn't stop to see himself, he is looking for something from you, he is like a mirror that wants to absorb, that's not true, the meaning of a word is its use in the language, there, laid out across the bonnet of the car, I am in my prime, chair on purple, those statues of legs in tights, responsive, desperate and fragile as they weave through the world, legs weave, yarn, criss cross, the storm, until she looks up, what rolling eye floats up gingerly, pond attached by a thread to the chair, standing in a circle of people, psychology functions as a point in the body, structuring the space of that body, and what about interiority, where is it, if I could read you like a book, if you were as transparent as water on your eye, beloved, "want to go for a paddle?", is reading a product of belief, goes neither backwards nor forwards, who owns you, it sticks to a single spot, from my bedroom, I eye you like a spider eyes a sky with its tiny facets of eye, inching, you've arrived in Schlump, would you like a side of schlump with your schlumpy attitude, schlumping, she attracted a lot of attention, she schlumped him for Jeremy, then Jeremy schlumped her for Zeffrey, I put my hands onto the material of the road, it could go anywhere, it could go here, into this piece of stain, it could enter into the tension of a neck, here, and lead the way into a pinch, do you ever feel this, are you writing about this now, are you feeling my thoughts, as if they were a scratch on the screen that faces you at night, when you are sad, were I alone again, stone home, the taps are running, what's a norm, flooding, so your mouth's compressed like lemons, I am, you say, but I still don't see, displacements are kinds of telescopes, fickle shortcuts covering the heads of strangers, heads of unknowing, I'm dumb, dramatic, thin, in the photo, on a tightrope, "I love you tons and tons and can't wait to see you again," I'm sick in bed again, she, stranded, somewhere here, touch too, is another kind of entrance, it offers a way of entry, even if that entry is as short as a surface, leafing, "the rooms are dimly lit, the chair is bare, the chinaware is gone," "the rooms are dimly lit, the furniture is gone," "the rooms are dimly lit, the walls are bare, the furniture is gone," too many buildings have fallen down, too much rubble has been heaped up, the moraines and deposits are insuperable, but I'm here, I don't think this is working, to pretend, I actually do the thing, I therefore have only pretended to pretend, or something like that, my conscious mind prefers to be a cut worm, it cut itself, this is its triumph, it forgives the plow because it is its own plow, not the cut worm forgives the plow, flowers grow everywhere so flowers are your eyes, field of vision is flowers, vision is a pistil, popping, wedge of object could be womb, could be room, structure of water is bent, going, beneath froth of feeling, blots of rubbed out parts like parts you forget, pale banana, I miss you, inside the tea, for you, remember it, the sea was rolling forever, on and on, the mind looking outside the body for some kind of sustenance, some sign of approval or distraction, get away, someone says, and other rooms out there, other wall, wall as good as shawl wrapping around my face at the table, voice trickles, fluffy rain, ruffles, moth-sized nibbling, clown lips, sky!, o photograph, you there, he/she staring back, squeeze into his/her periphery, make a circle and then break it, oh you, no, that window you can see into, Pierrot tan line, nose overwhelming one's mouth, Pierrot painted no depth other than wet, reflective surfaces, I like air baths, like Flaubert, do you like my boobs, invidious and homegrown, I see myself like the first time someone saw me, we sit across a table and eat green beans, is it more ethical to divest yourself of the body if you're a thinker, what is ruin, after all, I divulge my lack of eyebrows, smush face into camera, disappear, girls who do boys who do girls like they're boys who do boys like they're girls, accounts spilling all over the place, seen in tree, vast points in so many directions, please come here, spring has sprung, the observation is of course occurring, the nose is dipped in oxygen, the nose is suddenly free, bottle wire pinball pole dove outside streets bleat, your happiness is my happiness, I had hoped it would be a person with small slivers of teeth gleaming an excessive, highly artificial softness like the inside of a seashell that, despite its actual hardness, cannot ever live up to the word "hard," but is always misaligned with it, almost nearing the word "soft," about to, how touch and appearance are in conflict at times, what forms the artifact, commodity, and do you hear the donkey braying, face is like a diary I'm writing myself but also being written by, I'm into gum these days, gum can be compressed into crevices to enable wholeness, pop your mouth, something complete was ferreted away, potential bobbing under palates, speck, a little shop, we feel a milky stuffed feeling, weather, fiddles in chest, voice box clings to bread, shed, shred, she hired, destabilizing, his lobster, odds of depth, bobs of breath, sheep of splice, Brice likes mice, no small vest he could slip into, but enough, since there we are, you or I, without thought to ourselves, moving, when day is jammed into the room, jammed with flowers, my voice is the noise of work my voice pokes, already didn't know what your face looks like, but then in the evening I think I hide behind words or else place little mirrors around them like guards so that they don't reflect anything about me in them, so that they can be pure and self-referential, dream, such words can be the opposite of description, the opposite of portraiture, such words are, foliage scooped out, her breath, of, unknown on damp cheek, he is boiled and cold, I woke up this morning, fissure, what knots here, fib, wiggles a mop on the top of rose-brown, air fidgets with other air, the soul of finger wriggles out of itself, puffy with charm, I'm sort of embarrassed, impenetrable as a glass river surging into a dam's equally meaningless blue, as the Aer Lingus Boeing lugs its metal into air, lifting off the ground, "chicken or beef?", stare at grass spread thickly across a horizon, do you like phrases molded into the shape of an arrow, they can point to your innermost needled parts, where are they located, not clear, May arrives and carves out space for May, it seems, I'm just writing to you to let you know that outside my room there's a scent of eggs, and on my lap are remnants of shells, something broke open perhaps of its own accord, earth glass, I think earlier I must have visited the sea, maybe it was a river, it was obviously some body of water in any case, foot of dim wave, my body, what covers it, deepest I'd ever seen, my shirt like a sea, peak, peak, peek and, peak, peak, peek, and, violence, has an essence, it's trapped here in this container, one of its examples is the following ground made of stilts, pigeons of light, a single pigeon, again, you feel that comb-over sense of being, cafeteria, some version of curtains, triumphant in the center of the avenue, stolen identities, receipts, trash, hey you, the torch is in my hand, on the sagging upper deck, I think of heaping fraying heavy glossy squid on waves, everyone wants a "you," my body is slowing down because now I've reached that certain number of words, the engine sputters as it rubs up against the familiar, the familiar is a kind of rust, in the liquidity, repetition of things in which more of the same keeps pumping out, and yet, limbs and tributaries are quiet, staunch attempts against amputation, against change, via spill, water on wound, why we want to be framed by ourselves, in bread, bubbles of air make patterns of empty pockets in the flesh (flesh?) of dough, I listen to the others who speak, there is a hurdle around my inner ear that sounds can't jump over, instead they bounce off the slick rim and turn to a moist paste, all the sounds, suddenly, not to be able to hear, as in not to be able to absorb a portion of language that has been thrown one's way, so little swallows this non-silence that is not speech or locatable sound either, wishbone of a laugh, something sits on a fence, tender and singular, there is a bird too, and it is whole like a whole feeling, displaced into cartilage, here is a kind of crust, crust of feeling you are leaning on, strong and bewildered, there are people at the back of the bar, capes on stools, what translates to, sounds they make like some kind of pared-down description of a feeling that you are describing to yourself out loud under water, feel, feel, it is weak, it is a stern that keeps melting, keeps being measured, tucked into itself, by the size of a sea, sea comb, comb this feeling, comb it into a sea, sea is ripe, sea is chicken-colored, you are deeply frustrated by this, you had wanted so much to be free, you had wanted so much to be clear, you had wanted so much to become mutual with a room, or that sort of thing, with no taste, with a small single tooth to bite into anything, "well, my feeling is that," this thing that pivots on the string connecting the shaved atmosphere of waking and the sentiment, loosely I try to read something into what you are saying to me, what seems to rise into my head, or is it rinse it, it is raining, is it raining where you are, sweat around my eyes, highlighting my wrinkles, what the fuck is wrong with me, I mustn't forget to buy that cream on sale, on the decks of your eyes, tension between that which is blotted out and that which is highlighted, only more wasps flew in, or the ghost of the wasp multiplying itself with a vengeance, I closed the window, could make a stew tonight, the exercise is worth my while as long as it's useful, tiptoe of water, and I lie, lie in water and beside, imagine you're dragging a boar into a drawing patting its tail down in the page forgetting to include the snout, shimmies out, nausea can be a kind of hunger, can I fill nausea, all birds, I keep my phone close, like an eel out of water, faucet-faces yank us from stark sheets, atonal, red-nosed under folds, opposite the pour, yanked by bushy on the way to the bathroom, no more adjectives of objects blood-pecked and trickle of a water's hair pomade-pressed braid of a windpipe dragged up organic liquid, cannot slice a wave that rolls off mulberry thought tapping to the beat of my twin eyes stolen to make holes in the night of the disco, I have to sit down in the grass, softly, to contradict me, I could place this snickerdoodle, goldendoodle, cockapoo, cockatoo, cuddly but needy eye against my own, soul is a big tent, physical breath that skips, "what a curb is," while the disease of all my wanderings, tastes clipped, entropy is here on the sidewalk, lisp, foam, slug slides off of, imaginary seam, I could have loved, on the hinge of loving, of falling into it, I am looking into your window, I see you putting up your hair, I see your face in the mirror ballooning in my eye, I can see you say to yourself, is it going to be a good day, I can see you stand up, walk out of the other door, you are not late, they say, and I nod, is the sea heavy or light, are you heavy or light, you, ghost or spade, at times, chipped, a portentous world possesses him, meaning seems obvious and obscure at the same time, same characters as previous movement, her ears almost landing on surfaces, if, not committing to a single sound, dropping to the weight of gravity, minus the woman, plummet of an ear, impotent, the residue in form of what once had the possibility of not placing itself on the lip of a thing, of refusing sensation, shampoo, frizzy voice, fizzle, footnote, I saw a big space, I drew it, fell into it, bit of window, notes on the texture of paralysis, place an emotion into real glass, now take that same emotion and place it into an image of a glass, which instance gives the emotion a more defined contour, still, big true glob, utensil you can't use, of total grief, I brought it to the swimming pool, I'm lying in the hammock, suddenly I am salubrious, I glide on the lane like water and the gutters are scalps that need cleaning, opposite eye pours tear, it is soon dry, it does not blink with sense, squirms like a mackerel in teal, its tail for a second turning away from its eye's shiny black circle, glass, blowing all the way to horizons, bits of seeing caught in a fingernail, things, no cow, beautiful cow, he is me, when it is noon, often she goes out for air and stares at a blade of oxygen, she treats herself like clay, something that can keep bending, as water, structure of water is bent, if the sky is too small to fit, what, at the table, the external scene is there, you asked me what I was feeling, quite visible, poke spaghetti with spoon, twirling, this piece of traffic, it could enter into the tension of a neck, and lead the way to a pinch, and how it ripples sideways, words line up single file in the throat, the rest hiding in folds, big ideas were flowering, standing beside the cans of pineapple, I had been meaning to, less tin, fleshier, you will call me, a tip Thad tucked under his bagpipes, grey of grey, pear arms, pear arms, pear arms and ape, no pan, pale into hair, in a row with hats of song, song out of hats into grass, grass out of religion and into glass, glass is wrong, glass is so wrong on the weir glass is moor moor is more and heath for hire, hire is song song not higher but song bucket, disconnected fruit, more scene than astringent coo, more string than zebra, more stripe than stripe on circus burrito cone baby, and I am rigid, think of the air, how it can compress a plum-tint, egg onto icing egg tit and breaks sun, the residue in form of what once had the possibility of stinging, of being solid, could you have been, could you have been into it, could you have been into huge sprawling closeness of nerves, weight of nerves, white nerves you push out onto grass, nerves in grass, tap inside the noiseless tap, noiseless window tap, window is for tapping, window is winning in the weir, was swoon in the meadow, meadow as shadow, meadow as what should I eat, are you there, I don't want you to lose power, why can the bridge not suddenly turn into tables, or eyelashes, why can the chat not burst at the hem, and rub its unctuous glare, to talk is another form of knitting, feeble sweater, are you an obstacle you, what were we meant to be, what does it mean to be a resident, gluttonous desire to absolutely be consummated, to become, to be joined, and doesn't she, doesn't say anything, I get annoyed because I can't help anticipating a message coming maybe, hiccups, there are, tendrils of steam, I miss my train, catch it, sitting on a plumber steaming him like a Spanish leather shirt, or you, tender, green mirror black mirror grey mirror white mirror blue mirror red mirror yellow mirror, undoing, similarly, transport of ladders, we are making the body, we are all its parts fallen out like a waterfall, we collect it and scatter like a view of language, we are a life, there are lots of artist-intellectuals here sipping cheap wine, saying some interesting

.

things, a magician to finally pull a rabbit out of a hat of gaps, I want to believe, can you translate the way my finger wobbles with brie, ?, I am Donna Quixote, dimpled wheel used like a thought, it is just a slow horizontal fall like inside those tunnels in France, menstrual showers, stick in onions, feel, helmet, boomerang, emotion that accumulates a fatty density, only, dribbling eyes, what is the moment between thought and sensation I am looking for, a thought contains, is the idea of death the idea of completeness, our body, deflect spotty sky, rent as fern, space enters, open tinfoil, consciousness on face, psychic states are oil in water, yanked seedling inside jar, we found, with no water, but triangles, sorts of them, lost teensy flake of water, "want a bun?", "this is me, this is my life," taste toothpaste, what is the equivalent of feeling, miniature hairs that formerly stood on end begin to slacken, this is the arms, healthy unity of flesh in a car, what singular things congeal in heaps, sense beyond speech, or speech beyond sense, cell opens, flowers leak, flowers leak all over the place, and there is no metaphor, is there, just secretion, secretions of accents, a mountain plucked from your mouth like a scent, what almost is, a history without hands, but hands are there, this water is not clear, what part of you pours out, another type of grey, this is what we commerce in, the idea of day, and churning the milk of speech on the platform, weight clings to me where glass-life moves, no one's eyes tell you, the sheer physicality of what it entails, the feat of the body, to sew together disorder inside a cup of water, not supposed to be there, and, clearly, impossible to sew, roots into a thigh, say, steeping, fragments are, I know, all of us strung along, I would speak as each object in my dream for hours, sun, sun, I entered each thing diligently, sonar writing, who is you again, I you for you, give me a few you for you, bobbing you, I am sitting here, thinking everything that shrank in the roof of a mouth, having seen words, words congeal into icebergs that move up and down your face someone told me about, snap out of it, in light things fester, there before you, recently I, and all that, but more, and/or, and, door, curtain, open it, into the other, and out again, I'm so there, all over, with, in, out, off, who, under, or where, here, there, sea field, big open field, up, dimples etc., place in the field, field, field, more field.